BIOMES ON PLANET EARTH

MARINE BIOME

Kerri Mazzarella

Table of Contents

A Starfish Book

SEAHORSE PUBLISHING

Teaching Tips for Caregivers:

As a caregiver, you can help your child succeed in school by giving them a strong foundation in language and literacy skills and a desire to learn to read.

This book helps children grow by letting them practice reading skills.

Reading for pleasure and interest will help your child to develop reading skills and will give your child the opportunity to practice these skills in meaningful ways.

- Encourage your child to read on her own at home
- Encourage your child to practice reading aloud
- Encourage activities that require reading
- Establish a reading time
- Talk with your child
- Give your child writing materials

Teaching Tips for Teachers:

Research shows that one of the best ways for students to learn a new topic is to read about it.

Before Reading

- Read the "Words to Know" and discuss the meaning of each word.
- Read the back cover to see what the book is about.

During Reading

- When a student gets to a word that is unknown, ask them to look at the rest of the sentence to find clues to help with the meaning of the unknown word.
- Ask the student to write down any pages of the book that were confusing to them.

After Reading

- Discuss the main idea of the book.
- Ask students to give one detail that they learned in the book by showing a text dependent answer from the book.

MARINE BIOME

Earth has many kinds of areas that support life. These are called **biomes**.

Each biome has similar weather patterns, plants, and animals.

What is it like inside a marine biome?

Five oceans make up the marine biome.

If you split Earth's surface into ten equal parts, seven of them would be ocean.

DID YOU KNOW?

Earth's oceans are the Pacific, Atlantic, Indian, Southern, and Arctic.

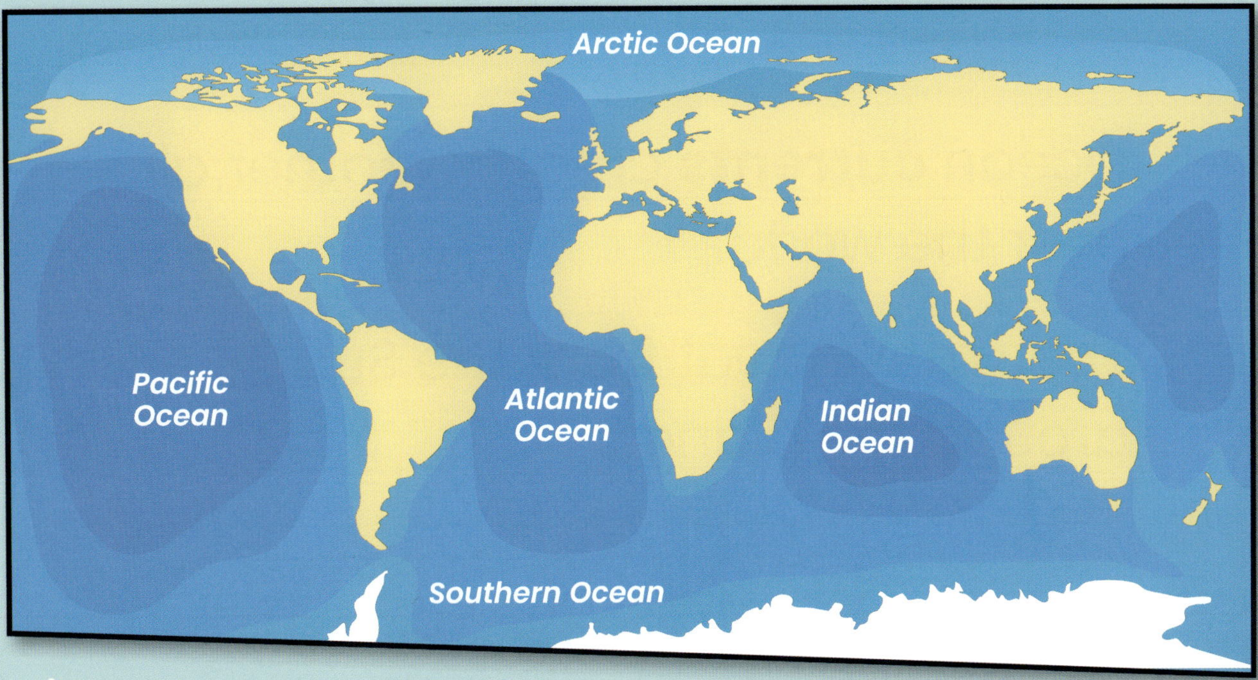
Arctic Ocean
Pacific Ocean
Atlantic Ocean
Indian Ocean
Southern Ocean

Ocean **currents** create weather all over the world.

They move heat from the Sun around the planet.

People need oceans.

We eat seafood.

We move supplies on ships.

DID YOU KNOW?

Kelp is the largest ocean plant. People eat kelp. Animals live in kelp forests.

People need oxygen to breathe.

Phytoplankton is the smallest ocean plant.

It makes almost half of all oxygen on Earth.

Oceans are full of life.

Tiny **coral polyps** build huge reefs.

Thousands of kinds of animals live around coral reefs.

DID YOU KNOW?

Scientists think that most ocean animals have not been discovered yet.

Big fish eat smaller fish.

Fish poop helps ocean plants grow.

DID YOU KNOW?

Fish can be shorter than one inch (three centimeters) and longer than 30 feet (nine meters).

Whales and other **mammals** rise to breathe air.

DID YOU KNOW?

The blue whale is the world's largest animal. It is bigger than two school buses!

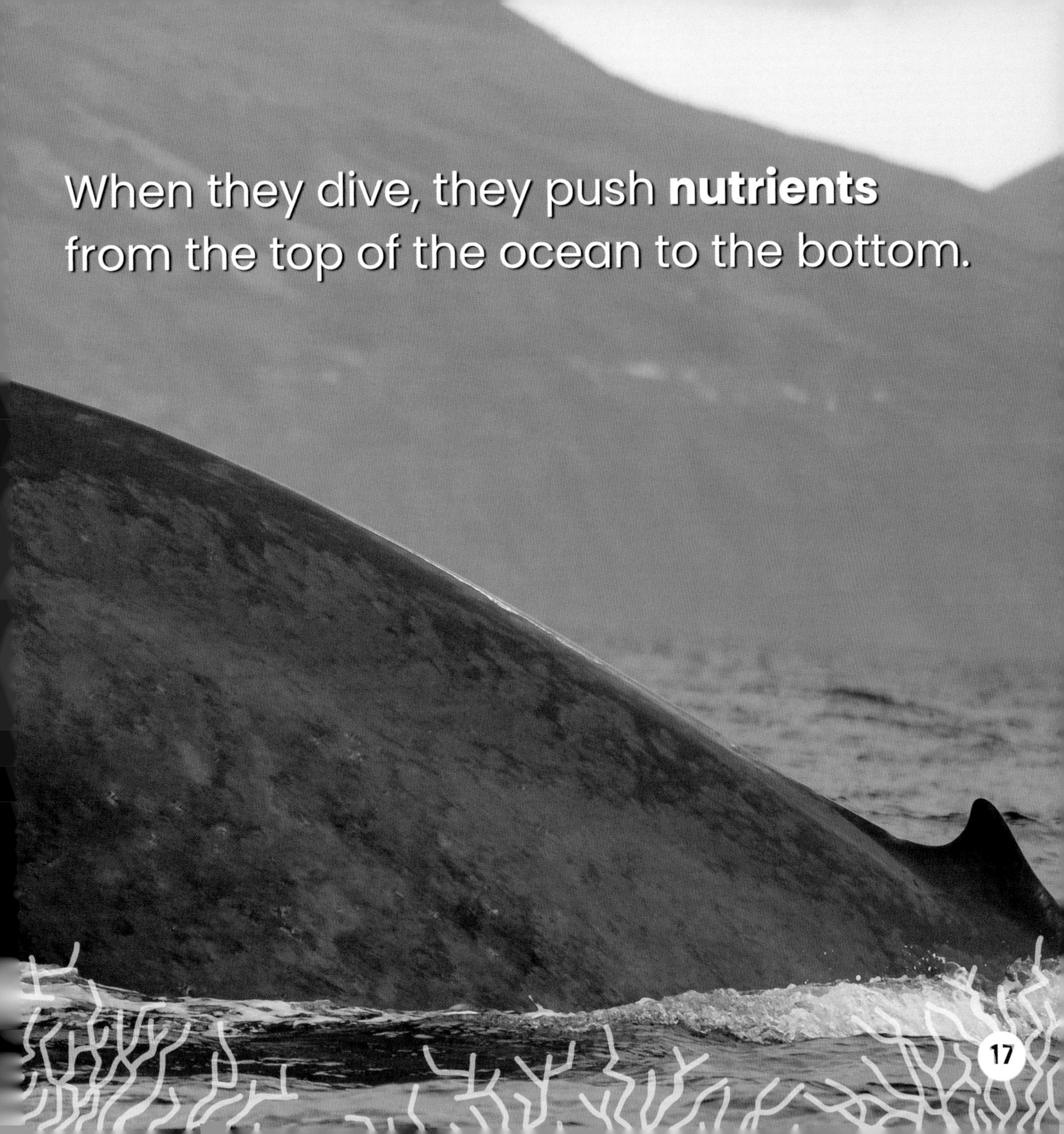

When they dive, they push **nutrients** from the top of the ocean to the bottom.

All living things in the marine biome work together for survival.

The marine biome is important for our planet.

How will you help protect it?

Words to Know

biomes (BYE-ohmz): large areas of similar ecosystems that share weather patterns, rainfall amounts, and types of plants and animals

coral polyps (KOR-uhl PAH-luhps): small ocean animals with tube-like bodies and round mouths surrounded by tentacles; the hard skeletons of coral polyp colonies join to form coral reefs

currents (KUR-uhnts): continuous movements of sea water driven by wind, waves, temperature, and other forces

mammals (MAM-uhlz): warm-blooded animals that have hair or fur, give birth to live young, and produce milk to feed their young; marine mammals include whales, seals, dolphins, and walruses

nutrients (NOO-tree-uhnts): materials, such as minerals or vitamins, which are needed for healthy growth

phytoplankton (FYE-toh-plangk-tuhn): microscopic plants that float near the surface of the ocean and provide food for many marine animals

Index

Comprehension Questions

1. What is the smallest ocean plant?
  a. kelp
  b. seafood
  c. phytoplankton

2. What builds coral reefs?
  a. coral polyps
  b. fish
  c. oxygen

3. Whales are
  a. fish.
  b. mammals.
  c. plants.

4. **True or false:** Big fish eat coral polyps.

5. **True or false:** People need to breathe oxygen.

Answers
1. c 2. a 3. b 4. False 5. True

About the Author

Kerri Mazzarella was born in New Hampshire and raised in South Florida. She graduated college from Florida State University. After college she worked in the school system as a Speech Language Pathologist. She has a love for children and is passionate about literacy and learning. She lives in South Florida with her husband, Chris. She has four children, and two dogs. They enjoy family time outside and love to travel.

Written by: Kerri Mazzarella
Design by: Kathy Walsh
Editor: Kim Thompson

Library of Congress PCN Data
Marine Biome / Kerri Mazzarella
Biomes on Planet Earth
ISBN 978-1-63897-468-0 (hard cover)
ISBN 978-1-63897-583-0 (paperback)
ISBN 978-1-63897-698-1 (EPUB)
ISBN 978-1-63897-813-8 (eBook)
Library of Congress Control Number: 2021953367

Printed in the United States of America.

Seahorse Publishing Company
www.seahorsepub.com

Published in the United States
Seahorse Publishing
PO Box 771325
Coral Springs, FL 33077

Photographs/Shutterstock: Cover & TOC: ©weera bunnak, ©ANTSTUDIO, ©korkeng, ©LilaloveDesign; Pg 4, 10, 11, 15, 16: ©GraphicStore; Pg 3-21: © LilaloveDesign; Pg 3: ©Drew McArthur; Pg 5: © Designua; Pg 6: ©FLX2; Pg 8: ©FOTOGRIN; Pg 10: ©Ethan Daniels; Pg 11: ©Choksawatdikorn; Pg 12: ©Solarisys; Pg 14: ©Najih_Walydh; Pg 15: ©VisionDive; Pg 16: ©Wild_and_free_naturephoto; Pg 18: ©Jacqueline Bodine; Pg 20: ©David Pereiras

SEAHORSE PUBLISHING